THE WILTSHIRE
COLOURING BOOK

First published 2016

The History Press
The Mill, Brimscombe Port
Stroud, Gloucestershire, GL5 2QG
www.thehistorypress.co.uk

Text © The History Press, 2016
Illustrations by Zak Kinnear & Kirsty Stewart © The History Press, 2016

British Library Cataloguing in Publication Data.
A catalogue record for this book is available from the British Library.

ISBN 978 0 7509 6810 2

Cover colouring by Lucy Hester.
Typesetting and origination by The History Press
Printed and bound in Great Britain by TJ International Ltd.

THE WILTSHIRE
COLOURING BOOK

PAST AND PRESENT

Take some time out of your busy life to relax and unwind with this
feel-good colouring book designed for everyone who loves Wiltshire.

Absorb yourself in the simple action of colouring in the scenes and settings from around the
county of Wiltshire, past and present. From Neolithic henges to picturesque villages, you are
sure to find some of your favourite locations waiting to be transformed with a splash of colour.

There are no rules – choose any page and any choice of colouring pens or pencils
you like to create your own unique, colourful and creative illustrations.

Lacock Abbey ▸

Corsham High Street ▶

Abbey House Gardens, Malmesbury ▸

Corsham Court ▸

Market Place, Chippenham, at the turn of the century ▶

Wadworth Brewery dray, Devizes ▸

Woodhenge, Amesbury ▸

Regent Street, Swindon, *c.* 1930 ▸

Avebury henge ▶

Bowood House and Gardens, Derry Hill ▸

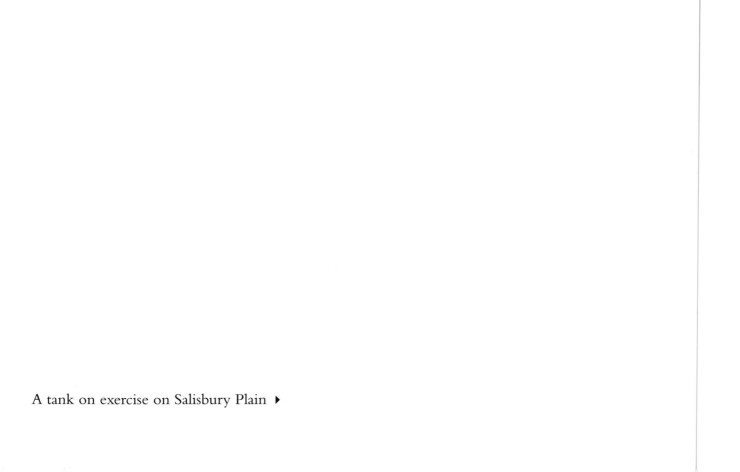

A tank on exercise on Salisbury Plain ▸

A butterfly at Longleat Safari Park ▸

Malmesbury Abbey ▸

Sailing on Shearwater Lake, Crockerton ▸

The ABC Savoy Cinema, Swindon, 1952 ▸

Racing on the Castle Combe Circuit ▸

Caen Hill Locks on the Kennet & Avon Canal ▸

Salisbury Cathedral ▶

Art deco diving board at Coate Water Country Park ▸

Castle Combe ▸

Old Wardour Castle, near Tisbury ▸

The New Inn, Salisbury ▸

Royal Wootton Bassett Old Town Hall ▸

A proud Wiltshire resident with his Austin 8 in 1953 ▸

Wiltshire Museum, Devizes ▸

The King's House, Salisbury Museum ▸

Westbury White Horse ▸

Church Street, Lacock ▸

Wilton Windmill ▸

Wilton House ▸

Stonehenge ▸

Stourhead House ▶

Swindon Speedway has a proud history ▸

The Courts Garden, Holt ▶

STEAM – Museum of the Great Western Railway, Swindon ▸

Bradford on Avon town bridge ▸

Old Sarum, Salisbury ▸

A barge on the Kennet & Avon Canal ▸

High Street, Marlborough, *c.* 1960s ▶

Earls hardware shop in Church Street, Trowbridge, 1958 ▸

Longleat House ▸

The Kennet & Avon Canal Museum, Devizes ▶

Longford Castle ▶

Great Chalfield Manor and Garden, Melksham ▸

Steam train on the Swindon and Cricklade Railway ▸

Also from The History Press

THE BRISTOL
COLOURING BOOK

PAST AND PRESENT

Find this colouring book and more at
www.thehistorypress.co.uk